The Anatomy of Faith

BernsPen

Published by BernsPen, 2026.

THE ANATOMY OF FAITH

First edition. January 12, 2026.

ISBN: 979-8233030901

Written by BernsPen.

Table of Contents

To every soul who has ever whispered a prayer, carried a hope, or trusted in tomorrow—this book is for you. May these reflections remind you that faith belongs to all of us, no matter where we come from or what we believe.

"Faith is the bird that feels the light and sings when the dawn is still dark." — Rabindranath Tagore

Introduction

Why Faith Still Matters

Faith is not a doctrine. It is not a rulebook. It is not a fixed answer to life's questions. Faith is a living presence—a pulse, a breath, a body in motion. It rises in silence, breaks in grief, heals in love, and stretches toward mystery.

This book is not about religion. It is about the anatomy of belief itself—the way trust lives in us, the way hope moves through us, the way love sustains us. Whether you call it faith, conviction, or simply the courage to keep going, this book invites you to explore what belief looks like from the inside out.

Drawing from psychology, neuroscience, and lived experience, *The Anatomy of Faith* maps the inner landscape of belief. Each chapter is a part of the body—a metaphor for how faith functions, falters, and finds renewal. You'll meet the pulse of trust, the breath of hope, the wounds of doubt, the healing of resilience, and the heart of love.

This is not a manual. It is a meditation. A conversation. A companion for those who have believed, stopped believing, or are learning to believe again.

You do not need certainty to begin. You only need curiosity. You do not need perfection. You only need presence. You do not need answers. You only need the willingness to listen to your own pulse.

Welcome to the anatomy of faith. May it meet you where you are—and carry you where you need to go.

Chapter 1: Faith as a Human Instinct

Faith begins not in temples or doctrines, but in the human mind itself. Psychologists often remind us that humans are *pattern-seeking creatures*. Our brains are wired to look for meaning, even in randomness. When we see the stars, we imagine constellations. When we hear thunder, we wonder about its cause. This instinct to connect dots, to trust that there is order beyond chaos, is the seed of faith.

Evolutionary psychology suggests that this tendency may have helped our ancestors survive. Believing that rustling in the bushes could be a predator—even if it wasn't—was safer than ignoring it. In other words, our brains evolved to assume intention and agency in the world around us. That same instinct is what allows us to believe in forces we cannot see, and to trust in futures we cannot yet touch.

Developmental psychology adds another layer. From birth, infants rely on faith—though they don't call it that yet. A baby reaching for a parent's arms doesn't know for certain they'll be caught, but they reach anyway. This is the foundation of *attachment theory*: trust built through repeated experiences of care. That trust becomes the heartbeat of resilience, shaping how we later approach relationships, hope, and belief.

Faith, then, is not just spiritual—it's biological, psychological, and universal. It's the instinct that allows us to step forward when the ground isn't fully visible. It's the quiet courage to believe in tomorrow, even when today feels uncertain.

And here's the beauty: faith doesn't belong to one religion, one race, or one culture. It belongs to humanity. Every community has found ways to express it—through stories, rituals, songs, or simply through acts of trust. Beneath all those differences lies the same instinct: the refusal to let despair have the final word.

So as we begin this anatomy, let's see faith not as doctrine, but as a human inheritance. It is the breath we all share, the pulse we all carry, the instinct that keeps us alive when certainty runs out.

Chapter 2: The Pulse of Faith

(Trust as the Heartbeat of Belief)

If faith is a living body, then trust is its heartbeat. It's the steady rhythm that keeps everything alive. Without trust, faith collapses. With trust, even the smallest flicker of hope can grow into something strong.

Psychologists often describe trust as the foundation of human connection. In developmental psychology, *attachment theory* shows us that infants learn to trust when caregivers respond consistently to their needs. That early rhythm of care—being fed when hungry, comforted when crying—becomes the heartbeat of resilience. It teaches us that the world can be safe, that people can be reliable, and that stepping forward is worth the risk.

Trust doesn't mean certainty. In fact, it often shows up when certainty is missing. We trust because we can't control everything. Social psychology reminds us that trust is what allows cooperation, community, and progress. Without it, relationships break down, societies fracture, and faith itself struggles to survive.

Of course, trust can be broken. We've all felt the sting of betrayal, the ache of disappointment. Research in trauma psychology shows that broken trust can lead to withdrawal, anxiety, or even cynicism. But here's the hopeful part: trust can be rebuilt. Slowly, carefully, like a heartbeat returning after silence. Studies on resilience suggest that people who rebuild trust after loss often develop deeper, more authentic connections than before.

Trust is not blind. It's not about ignoring reality or pretending everything will be fine. It's about choosing to believe in possibilities, even when the evidence isn't complete. Psychologists call this *risk-based trust*:

the willingness to invest in relationships or futures despite uncertainty. It's the courage to say: *I will risk hope, because hope is worth the risk.*

So when we talk about the anatomy of faith, let's remember this: trust is the pulse that keeps faith alive. It beats quietly in the background of our lives, reminding us that even in uncertainty, we can still move, still love, still believe.

Chapter 3: The Breath of Faith

(Hope as Oxygen)

If trust is the heartbeat of faith, then hope is its breath. Just as our lungs draw in oxygen to keep us alive, hope fills us with the strength to keep moving forward. Without hope, faith suffocates. With hope, even the darkest night feels a little less heavy.

Psychologists often describe hope as more than just wishful thinking. In positive psychology, Charles Snyder's *hope theory* explains that hope is built on two things: the belief that goals can be achieved, and the pathways we imagine to reach them. In other words, hope is both vision and strategy—it's the breath that keeps us alive and moving.

Think about the times you've faced uncertainty. Waiting for medical results. Hoping for a job interview to go well. Standing at the edge of loss, wondering how to keep going. In those moments, hope is the breath that steadies us. It doesn't erase pain or fear, but it gives us enough air to take the next step.

Research shows that hope is a powerful predictor of resilience. People with higher levels of hope tend to recover faster from setbacks, adapt more easily to change, and even experience better physical health. Martin Seligman, one of the founders of positive psychology, calls this *learned optimism*—the ability to train ourselves to breathe hope even when circumstances feel suffocating.

Hope is universal. It doesn't belong to one culture or one religion—it belongs to humanity. A farmer planting seeds trusts the soil, but it's hope that makes them believe in the harvest. A student opening a book trusts their effort, but it's hope that makes them believe in a future. A parent watching their child sleep trusts the night, but it's hope that makes them believe in tomorrow.

Of course, hope can feel fragile. Sometimes it's just a whisper, a flicker, a single breath in a storm. But even the smallest breath matters. It keeps us alive long enough to see change, long enough to discover resilience we didn't know we had.

Hope doesn't deny reality—it transforms it. It says: *Yes, the night is long, but dawn will come.* It says: *Yes, the struggle is real, but so is the possibility of renewal.* Hope is the oxygen of faith, and without it, we cannot survive the weight of uncertainty.

So breathe deeply. Let hope fill your lungs. Let it remind you that even in the hardest seasons, faith is not about knowing the outcome—it's about believing that life is still worth living.

Chapter 4: The Mind of Faith

(Doubt as Companion)

We often think of doubt as the enemy of faith, but psychology suggests it may be one of its closest companions. Faith without questions can become rigid, brittle. Doubt keeps faith alive, flexible, and honest. It's the mind of faith—the part that asks, *Why? How? What if?*

Cognitive psychology tells us that doubt is a natural response to uncertainty. Our brains are wired to resolve tension between what we believe and what we experience—a process known as *cognitive dissonance*. When reality doesn't match expectation, doubt steps in. And while that tension can feel uncomfortable, it's also what pushes us to grow, adapt, and refine our beliefs.

Developmental psychology echoes this. Jean Piaget's theory of cognitive development shows that questioning is essential for learning. Children don't just accept the world as it is—they poke, prod, and ask "why" endlessly. That curiosity, that doubt, is what allows them to build deeper understanding. Adults are no different. Our doubts force us to re-examine, to stretch, to evolve.

Of course, doubt can feel unsettling. It shakes the ground beneath our feet, leaving us unsure of what to hold onto. But research in resilience psychology suggests that people who wrestle with doubt often emerge with stronger, more authentic convictions. Faith that has been tested by questions is more durable than faith that has never been challenged.

Here's the paradox: the more we allow doubt, the more real our faith becomes. When we admit we don't have all the answers, we open ourselves to mystery. When we wrestle with uncertainty, we discover resilience. Doubt doesn't weaken faith—it makes it human.

So let's not fear doubt. Let's see it as a companion walking beside us, asking questions that sharpen our vision. Faith is not the absence of doubt—it's the courage to keep believing in the presence of it.

Chapter 5: The Bones of Faith

(Stories and Traditions as Structure)

If faith is a living body, then stories and traditions are its bones. They give shape, structure, and stability to something that might otherwise feel intangible. Without bones, the body collapses. Without stories, faith drifts.

Psychologists who study *narrative psychology* remind us that humans are storytelling creatures. We don't just live events—we weave them into narratives that help us make sense of life. Dan McAdams, a leading voice in this field, describes identity itself as a "life story." We remember, retell, and reinterpret our experiences until they form a framework we can stand on. That framework is what gives faith its structure.

Across cultures, traditions act like scaffolding. Rituals, songs, myths, and communal practices are not just cultural artifacts—they are psychological anchors. They remind us that we belong to something larger than ourselves. Anthropologists and psychologists alike note that rituals reduce anxiety, strengthen social bonds, and provide continuity in times of change. In moments of uncertainty, traditions are the bones that hold us upright.

Think about the stories you grew up with. Maybe they were religious parables, family legends, or cultural myths. Even if you no longer believe them literally, they shaped your sense of meaning. They gave you a skeleton to build your identity around. And when life feels chaotic, those bones remind you that you are part of a larger human story.

Of course, bones can be rigid. Sometimes traditions feel heavy, restrictive, or outdated. Psychology acknowledges this tension: while structure provides stability, too much rigidity can stifle growth. That's why faith must balance bones with breath, pulse, and mind. Stories and traditions give us something to hold onto, but they must also evolve, flex, and adapt to new generations.

Chapter 6: The Hands of Faith

(Action and Service)

Faith is not only something we feel—it's something we do. If trust is the heartbeat and hope is the breath, then action is the hands of faith. It's how belief moves from the invisible to the visible, from the inner world to the outer one.

Psychologists often remind us that behavior shapes belief just as much as belief shapes behavior. Albert Bandura's *social learning theory* shows that we learn not only by thinking, but by watching and doing. When we act with kindness, generosity, or courage, those actions reinforce our sense of meaning. Faith becomes real when it is lived.

Think about the small acts of service you've seen or given. A neighbor sharing food during hard times. A stranger offering directions when you're lost. A friend showing up when you least expect it. These are not grand gestures, but they are the hands of faith at work—reminders that belief is not just about what we hold inside, but how we extend ourselves outward.

Behavioral psychology adds another layer. B.F. Skinner's work on reinforcement suggests that actions repeated and rewarded become habits. In the same way, acts of compassion strengthen faith. Each time we choose generosity over indifference, we reinforce the belief that goodness matters. Over time, service becomes not just something we do, but part of who we are.

Of course, action can be costly. Serving others requires time, energy, and sometimes sacrifice. But research in positive psychology shows that altruism often increases well-being. Helping others doesn't just benefit them—it strengthens our own resilience, deepens our sense of purpose, and reminds us that faith is not a solitary journey.

Chapter 7: The Voice of Faith

(Prayer, Poetry, and Expression)

Faith doesn't just live in silence—it speaks. Sometimes softly, sometimes boldly, sometimes in words, sometimes in song. If the hands of faith are action, then the voice of faith is expression. It's how belief finds language, how hope becomes audible, how trust is shared.

Psychologists who study *expressive writing* and *language psychology* remind us that putting feelings into words changes how we experience them. James Pennebaker's research shows that writing about emotions can reduce stress, improve health, and help us make sense of difficult experiences. In the same way, prayer, poetry, and storytelling give faith a voice—they help us process uncertainty and transform it into meaning.

Across cultures, faith has always spoken through ritual words, chants, hymns, and poetry. These aren't just artistic flourishes—they are psychological tools. Language creates rhythm, repetition, and imagery that soothe the mind and strengthen belief. Neuroscience even shows that reciting or singing can calm the nervous system, lowering anxiety and reinforcing a sense of connection.

Think about the times you've given voice to faith. Whispering a prayer in the dark. Singing along to a song that carried you through heartbreak. Reading a poem that seemed to put your own unspoken feelings into words. In those moments, faith wasn't just an idea—it was alive, breathing through your voice.

Of course, not everyone expresses faith the same way. For some, it's prayer. For others, it's poetry, music, or even conversation. Psychology calls this *self-expression*, and it's one of the most powerful ways humans regulate emotion. When we give voice to what we believe, we strengthen it—not only for ourselves, but for those who hear us.

Chapter 8: The Eyes of Faith

(Vision and Imagination)

Faith is not only about what we feel or do—it's also about how we see. If the hands of faith are action and the voice of faith is expression, then the eyes of faith are vision. They allow us to look beyond what is visible, to imagine possibilities that have not yet arrived.

Psychologists who study *imagination and perception* remind us that the human brain is not limited to what the senses provide. Neuroscience shows that when we imagine something vividly, the same regions of the brain activate as if we were actually seeing it. This means vision is not just about sight—it's about the mind's ability to picture futures, hopes, and possibilities. Faith thrives in that space.

Hope researchers often describe imagination as the "visual arm" of belief. Charles Snyder's *hope theory* emphasizes that people who can envision pathways toward their goals are more likely to achieve them. In other words, the eyes of faith don't just see what is—they see what could be.

Think about the times you've used imagination as a form of faith. A student picturing themselves graduating, even when the road feels long. A patient imagining recovery, even when illness weighs heavy. A community envisioning justice, even when oppression seems overwhelming. These visions are not fantasies—they are acts of faith, shaping reality by first shaping perception.

Of course, vision can be distorted. Psychology warns us about *confirmation bias*—the tendency to see only what we want to see. Faith must balance vision with humility, remembering that imagination is powerful but not infallible. The eyes of faith must stay open, not only to dreams but also to truth.

Yet when vision is clear, it becomes a compass. It directs our steps, sustains our hope, and strengthens our trust. Faith without vision is blind; faith with vision can see beyond the horizon.

Chapter 9: The Path of Faith

(Journeys and Everyday Steps)

Faith is not only about what we feel inside—it's about how we move through the world. If the eyes of faith give us vision, then the path of faith is the journey itself: the steps we take each day, the choices we make, the direction we follow even when the road is uncertain.

Psychologists who study *goal-setting* remind us that progress often comes in small, consistent steps rather than dramatic leaps. Edwin Locke and Gary Latham's research on *goal-setting theory* shows that clear, purposeful goals motivate us to keep moving forward, even when obstacles appear. Faith works in much the same way—it gives us a sense of direction, a path to walk, even when we don't know exactly where it will lead.

Think about the journeys you've taken in your own life. Maybe it was pursuing an education, starting a family, healing from loss, or building a dream. None of those paths were straight. They twisted, turned, and sometimes seemed to vanish altogether. Yet faith is what kept you walking. It's the quiet belief that each step matters, even when the destination isn't visible.

Resilience psychology adds another layer. Studies show that people who frame life as a journey rather than a fixed outcome are better able to adapt to change. They see setbacks not as failures, but as detours. This mindset—sometimes called *pathway thinking*—is central to hope theory. It's the ability to imagine alternate routes when the road ahead is blocked. Faith thrives in this flexibility.

Of course, the path of faith is not always easy. There are seasons when the road feels endless, when fatigue sets in, when doubt whispers that it's not worth continuing. But psychology reminds us that perseverance—what Angela Duckworth calls *grit*—is often the difference between giving up and breaking through. Faith fuels grit. It gives us the courage to keep walking, even when the journey feels long.

Chapter 10: The Silence of Faith

(Stillness and Mystery)

Not all faith is spoken. Not all faith is acted out. Sometimes, faith lives in silence. If the voice of faith is expression, then the silence of faith is stillness—the quiet space where belief rests, where mystery breathes, where we learn to listen.

Psychologists who study *mindfulness* remind us that silence is not emptiness—it is presence. Research shows that practices of stillness, such as meditation or contemplative prayer, reduce stress, calm the nervous system, and increase emotional resilience. In silence, the mind shifts from constant noise to gentle awareness. Faith often grows strongest in that quiet space.

Neuroscience adds another layer. Studies on the brain's *default mode network* reveal that when we are still, our minds wander inward—reflecting, imagining, and connecting past experiences with future possibilities. This inward turn is not wasted time; it is the brain's way of integrating meaning. Silence, then, becomes a laboratory for faith, where questions and hopes are processed beneath the surface.

Think about the moments when silence carried you. Sitting in a hospital waiting room. Standing at a graveside. Watching the sunrise alone. In those moments, words failed, but faith did not. Silence became the language of trust, the breath of hope, the companion of doubt.

Of course, silence can feel uncomfortable. Many of us rush to fill it with words, music, or distraction. Psychology calls this *avoidance coping*—the tendency to escape discomfort rather than face it. Yet when we resist that urge and stay with silence, we often discover something deeper: a sense of mystery, of connection, of faith that doesn't need explanation.

Chapter 11: The Wounds of Faith

(Loss and Crisis)

Faith is not immune to pain. Just as the body can be wounded, so can belief. Loss, betrayal, tragedy—these moments cut deep, leaving scars that challenge the very foundations of trust and hope. If faith is a living body, then wounds are the places where it bleeds.

Psychologists who study *trauma and resilience* remind us that crises often shake our deepest assumptions. Janoff-Bulman's theory of *shattered assumptions* explains that trauma disrupts our basic beliefs: that the world is safe, that life is fair, that tomorrow will resemble today. When those assumptions collapse, faith feels fractured.

Think about the moments when faith was wounded in your own life. The death of someone you loved. A betrayal that left you questioning trust. A crisis that made you wonder if hope was worth holding onto. In those moments, faith doesn't disappear—but it limps, it falters, it struggles to breathe.

Yet psychology also shows that wounds can become openings. Viktor Frankl, a Holocaust survivor and psychiatrist, developed *logotherapy*, the idea that meaning is the key to survival. He argued that even in suffering, humans can find purpose—and that purpose becomes the seed of renewed faith. This is what researchers call *post-traumatic growth*: the ability to emerge from crisis with deeper resilience, stronger relationships, and a clearer sense of meaning.

Of course, wounds leave scars. Faith after loss is never the same as faith before it. But scars are not signs of weakness—they are signs of healing. They remind us that faith has been tested, broken, and rebuilt. And often, the rebuilt faith is more authentic, more compassionate, more human.

Chapter 12: The Healing of Faith

(Renewal and Resilience)

Every living body has the capacity to heal, and so does faith. If wounds mark the places where belief has been broken, then healing is the process by which faith learns to live again—sometimes scarred, but often stronger.

Psychologists who study *resilience* remind us that healing is not about erasing pain, but about integrating it. George Bonanno's research on resilience shows that most people, even after trauma, find ways to adapt and recover. Healing is not linear—it comes in waves, in small steps, in moments of renewal that slowly rebuild trust and hope.

Meaning-making is central to this process. Viktor Frankl's *logotherapy* argued that humans can endure almost any suffering if they can find meaning within it. Modern psychology echoes this: people who interpret loss as part of a larger story often experience *post-traumatic growth*. They emerge with deeper compassion, stronger relationships, and a clearer sense of purpose. Healing, then, is not just recovery—it is transformation.

Think about the ways faith heals in everyday life. A grieving parent who plants a tree in memory of their child. A community rebuilding after disaster, finding strength in shared rituals. An individual who, after betrayal, learns to trust again—slowly, carefully, but with renewed depth. These acts of renewal are the healing hands of faith at work.

Neuroscience adds another layer. Studies on *neuroplasticity* show that the brain can rewire itself after trauma, forming new pathways of thought and emotion. Healing is not only spiritual—it is biological. Each act of resilience, each moment of meaning-making, literally reshapes the brain, allowing faith to grow in new directions.

Of course, healing takes time. It cannot be rushed or forced. Psychology reminds us that recovery is often uneven—two steps forward, one step back. But even in setbacks, healing continues. The scars remain, but they become reminders of survival, of strength, of faith that endured.

Chapter 13: The Legacy of Faith

(Passing Belief Across Generations)

Faith is not only something we carry—it's something we pass on. If the bones of faith give it structure and the hands of faith give it action, then legacy is the way faith moves beyond us, into the lives of those who come after.

Psychologists who study *intergenerational memory* remind us that beliefs, values, and traditions are often transmitted through stories, rituals, and everyday practices. Social identity theory adds that belonging to a group—whether family, culture, or community—shapes how we see ourselves and what we believe. Faith, then, is not just personal; it is communal, woven into the fabric of identity across generations.

Think about the ways faith has been handed down in your own life. A grandparent's prayer whispered at bedtime. A family story told around the table. A cultural ritual practiced year after year. These moments are more than habits—they are acts of transmission, carrying belief from one heart to another.

Developmental psychology shows that children learn not only through instruction but through observation. Albert Bandura's *social learning theory* explains that we imitate what we see. When young people witness acts of kindness, resilience, or hope, they internalize those behaviors as part of their own faith. Legacy is not just taught—it is modeled.

Of course, legacy can change. Sometimes new generations question or reshape the beliefs they inherit. This is not a rejection of faith but a renewal of it. Psychology calls this *identity negotiation*—the process of balancing tradition with individuality. In this way, faith evolves, adapting to new contexts while still honoring its roots.

Legacy is not about perfection. It's about presence. It's about leaving behind not just words, but lived examples of trust, hope, and resilience. Research on *generativity*—a concept from Erik Erikson's stages of development—shows that adults find meaning in guiding the next generation. Passing on faith, in whatever form, is one of the deepest ways we participate in that generativity.

Chapter 14: The Horizon of Faith

(Future and Transformation)

Faith is not only about the past we inherit or the present we live—it is also about the future we imagine. If the eyes of faith give us vision, then the horizon of faith is where that vision stretches outward, toward transformation. It is the place where belief meets possibility, where hope becomes anticipation, where trust leans into tomorrow.

Psychologists who study *future orientation* remind us that the ability to imagine and plan for the future is one of humanity's greatest strengths. Research shows that people who think ahead—who set goals, anticipate challenges, and envision possibilities—are more resilient in the face of uncertainty. Faith thrives in this forward-looking posture. It is not just about surviving today; it is about believing in tomorrow.

Resilience psychology adds another layer. Studies on *anticipatory resilience* suggest that preparing for future challenges, even before they arrive, strengthens our ability to endure them. Faith often works this way—it gives us the courage to face what has not yet happened, to trust that even in the unknown, we will find strength.

Think about the horizons you've looked toward in your own life. The dream of a new career. The hope of healing after loss. The vision of a community transformed by justice or compassion. These horizons are not guarantees, but they are anchors. They remind us that the future is not fixed—it is shaped by the choices we make today.

Of course, the horizon can feel distant. Sometimes the future seems too uncertain, too overwhelming, too far away to grasp. Psychology warns us about *future anxiety*—the tendency to worry about what might go wrong. But faith reframes that anxiety into anticipation. It says: *Yes, the future is unknown, but it is also open. Yes, tomorrow is uncertain, but it is also full of possibility.*

Transformation is the gift of the horizon. Faith does not promise that the future will be easy, but it does promise that the future can be different. And in that difference lies hope, renewal, and growth.

Chapter 15: The Community of Faith

(Belonging and Connection)

Faith is not only personal—it is shared. If the path of faith is the journey we walk, then the community of faith is the company we keep along the way. Belonging gives faith strength, connection gives it warmth, and togetherness gives it resilience.

Psychologists who study *social bonds* remind us that humans are wired for connection. Social identity theory explains that belonging to a group shapes how we see ourselves and what we believe. Faith, then, is not just an individual conviction—it is a collective experience, reinforced by the presence of others.

Research on *collective resilience* shows that communities facing hardship often endure better together than alone. Shared rituals, mutual support, and collective meaning-making help people recover from crises more quickly. Faith thrives in this communal space—it becomes not just "my belief," but "our belief," carried by many voices and many hands.

Think about the times when community sustained you. A congregation singing together. A neighborhood rebuilding after disaster. A circle of friends offering comfort in grief. In those moments, faith was not solitary—it was shared, multiplied, strengthened by connection.

Of course, communities are not perfect. They can wound as well as heal, exclude as well as embrace. Psychology acknowledges this tension: while belonging provides identity and support, it can also create division if boundaries become rigid. That is why healthy communities of faith must balance tradition with openness, identity with inclusivity.

Yet when community is strong, it becomes one of the most powerful expressions of faith. It reminds us that belief is not only about what we hold inside—it is about what we share, what we build, what we sustain together.

Chapter 16: The Heart of Faith

(Love as Core Energy)

At the center of faith lies love. If trust is the pulse, hope the breath, and community the body, then love is the energy that animates it all. Without love, faith becomes hollow. With love, faith becomes alive—radiant, resilient, and transformative.

Psychologists who study *attachment* remind us that love begins as a bond. From infancy, secure attachment provides the foundation for trust, resilience, and emotional health. John Bowlby's work shows that when caregivers respond with warmth and consistency, children develop not only security but also the capacity to love others. Faith, in many ways, grows from this same soil: the experience of being held, cared for, and valued.

Compassion research adds another dimension. Kristin Neff's studies on *self-compassion* reveal that treating ourselves with kindness reduces anxiety, increases resilience, and strengthens our ability to extend love outward. Faith rooted in love is not only about loving others—it is also about loving ourselves, recognizing our worth, and embracing our humanity.

Altruism, too, is central. Positive psychology shows that acts of love—whether through generosity, service, or empathy—create a feedback loop of well-being. Helping others doesn't just benefit them; it nourishes us, reinforcing the belief that life is meaningful. Faith expressed through love becomes both a gift and a renewal.

Think about the moments when love carried you. A friend who stayed by your side in grief. A parent's sacrifice. A stranger's kindness that arrived just when you needed it. These are not just gestures—they are the heart of faith beating in the world, reminding us that belief is not abstract but embodied in love.

Of course, love is not always easy. It requires vulnerability, risk, and sometimes forgiveness. Psychology acknowledges that love can wound as well as heal. Yet even in its fragility, love remains the most powerful energy of faith. It is what allows us to trust again after betrayal, to hope again after loss, to believe again after doubt.

Chapter 17: The Mindfulness of Faith

(Presence and Awareness)

Faith is not only about the past we remember or the future we imagine—it is also about the present we inhabit. If the horizon of faith stretches forward, then mindfulness is the grounding force that keeps us here, now. Presence is the soil where faith takes root, awareness the light that helps it grow.

Psychologists who study *mindfulness* remind us that being present is not passive—it is active attention. Jon Kabat-Zinn, a pioneer in mindfulness-based stress reduction, defines mindfulness as "paying attention in a particular way: on purpose, in the present moment, and nonjudgmentally." Faith thrives in this posture. It is not about escaping reality, but about inhabiting it fully.

Research on *flow states* adds another dimension. Mihaly Csikszentmihalyi's work shows that when we are deeply absorbed in meaningful activity, we experience joy, clarity, and timelessness. Faith often feels like this flow: a sense of being carried, of aligning with something larger than ourselves, of losing track of fear because presence is enough.

Think about the moments when mindfulness carried you. Sitting quietly with a cup of tea. Walking slowly through nature. Listening deeply to someone's story without rushing to respond. In those moments, faith was not about answers or outcomes—it was about awareness, about being fully alive in the present.

Of course, presence can be difficult. Our minds wander to regrets of the past or anxieties about the future. Psychology calls this *rumination* and *anticipatory worry*. Yet mindfulness practices—breathing, meditation, prayer, or simply pausing—help us return to now. And in the now, faith finds its strength.

Chapter 18: The Mystery of Faith

(Transcendence and the Unknown)

Faith is not only about what we know—it is also about what we cannot know. If mindfulness grounds us in presence, then mystery lifts us into transcendence. Mystery is the horizon we cannot cross, the silence we cannot explain, the unknown that humbles us and yet draws us closer.

Psychologists who study *awe and transcendence* remind us that encountering the vast and unexplainable often transforms us. Research by Dacher Keltner and Jonathan Haidt shows that experiences of awe—standing before a mountain, gazing at the stars, hearing music that moves us—expand our perception of time, increase compassion, and deepen our sense of belonging. Faith thrives in awe because awe reminds us that we are part of something larger than ourselves.

Existential psychology adds another layer. Viktor Frankl argued that life's deepest meaning often emerges not from certainty, but from mystery. The unknown forces us to wrestle with questions of purpose, mortality, and transcendence. Faith does not erase these questions—it embraces them, allowing mystery to become a source of wonder rather than fear.

Think about the moments when mystery carried you. Watching the ocean stretch endlessly. Holding a newborn child and marveling at life. Standing in grief, yet sensing something beyond loss. In those moments, faith was not about answers—it was about presence in the unknown, about trusting that mystery itself has meaning.

Of course, mystery can unsettle us. Psychology notes that humans crave control and predictability; uncertainty often triggers anxiety. Yet when we allow mystery to remain—when we stop demanding explanations—we often discover peace. Faith teaches us that not everything must be solved; some truths are meant to be lived, not explained.

Chapter 19: The Death and Rebirth of Faith

(Cycles of Renewal)

Faith, like life, moves in cycles. It is born, it grows, it falters, it dies—and sometimes, it is reborn. If the wounds of faith mark its breaking, then rebirth marks its renewal. Death is not the end of faith; it is often the beginning of transformation.

Psychologists who study *identity reconstruction* remind us that crises often force us to let go of old identities and rebuild new ones. After loss, betrayal, or disillusionment, people often experience what researchers call *transformational change.* This is not simply recovery—it is the creation of a new self, a new way of believing, a new way of living. Faith follows this same rhythm.

Think about the times when faith seemed to die in your own life. Perhaps a belief you held no longer fit reality. Perhaps a tradition felt empty. Perhaps hope itself seemed impossible. In those moments, faith felt gone. Yet often, something new emerged—a deeper, more authentic belief, reshaped by struggle.

Existential psychology emphasizes this paradox. Rollo May wrote that "the courage to be" often requires facing nothingness—the death of old certainties—before new meaning can arise. Faith, then, is not destroyed by death; it is refined by it. The ashes of old belief become the soil for new growth.

Post-traumatic growth research echoes this. People who endure profound loss often report not only recovery, but renewal: a stronger sense of purpose, deeper compassion, and greater appreciation for life. Faith reborn after death is often more resilient, more human, more grounded in reality.

Of course, rebirth is not easy. It requires surrender, humility, and patience. Psychology reminds us that transformation takes time—old identities must be mourned before new ones can be embraced. But when rebirth comes, it is powerful. It is faith that has been tested, broken, and remade.

Chapter 20: The Wholeness of Faith

(Integration and Balance)

Faith is not just a collection of parts—it is a whole. The pulse, the breath, the bones, the hands, the voice, the eyes, the path, the silence, the wounds, the healing, the legacy, the horizon, the community, the heart, the mindfulness, and the mystery—all of these are pieces of a living body. Wholeness is what happens when they come together in balance.

Psychologists who study *self-integration* remind us that well-being depends on coherence. Carl Rogers described the "fully functioning person" as someone whose inner experiences align with their outer actions. Faith works in the same way: when belief, practice, emotion, and community are integrated, faith becomes whole. Fragmentation leads to confusion; integration leads to strength.

Positive psychology adds another dimension. Martin Seligman's *PERMA model* of well-being—Positive emotion, Engagement, Relationships, Meaning, and Accomplishment—shows that flourishing requires balance across multiple domains. Faith, too, flourishes when it integrates joy, service, belonging, meaning, and growth. Wholeness is not perfection—it is harmony.

Think about the times when faith felt whole in your life. A moment of prayer that led to action. A wound that led to healing. A tradition that connected you to community while also opening you to mystery. In those moments, faith was not fragmented—it was integrated, balanced, alive.

Of course, wholeness is never static. Psychology reminds us that integration is a process, not a destination. Life shifts, beliefs evolve, communities change. Faith must continually re-balance, re-integrate, re-align. Wholeness is not about holding everything tightly—it is about allowing the parts to work together, even as they grow.

Epilogue: Carrying Faith Forward

Faith, like life, is never finished. We have traced its anatomy—the pulse, the breath, the wounds, the healing, the community, the heart, the wholeness. Each part reveals something essential, yet together they remind us that faith is not a static body but a living presence.

The journey through these chapters has shown that faith is both fragile and resilient, both personal and communal, both grounded and transcendent. It is shaped by psychology, nourished by love, tested by loss, renewed by healing, and carried forward in legacy.

But the anatomy of faith is not only a map—it is an invitation. An invitation to notice the pulse of trust in your own life. To breathe hope when despair feels heavy. To walk the path with resilience. To honor silence, mystery, and community. To let love be the heart that sustains you.

Faith will continue to evolve, as it always has. It will die and be reborn, it will fracture and be healed, it will stretch toward horizons we cannot yet see. And in every cycle, it will remind us that belief is not about certainty—it is about meaning, presence, and connection.

So carry faith forward—not as a finished anatomy, but as a living body. Let it grow, let it change, let it breathe. And may it remind you, in every season, that even in the unknown, there is always a pulse of trust, a breath of hope, and a heart of love.

Recommended Books & Articles

1. Faith from a Positive Psychology Perspective

- **Authors**: Cindy Miller-Perrin & Elizabeth Krumrei Mancuso
- **Publisher**: Springer Nature
- **Focus**: Explores how religious faith contributes to optimal psychological functioning, well-being, and resilience.
- **Highlights**:
- Integrates international and cross-cultural perspectives
- Discusses faith through the lens of positive psychology
- Useful for understanding faith as a strength-based psychological resource
- Read on Springer

2. The Role of Faith in Psychological Resilience

- **Source**: iResearchNet (Transpersonal Psychology)
- **Focus**: Examines how both religious and secular belief systems help individuals cope with adversity.
- **Highlights**:
- Differentiates positive vs. negative religious coping

- Explores trauma recovery and post-traumatic growth
- Discusses cultural variations in faith-based resilience
- Read the article

3. Top 10 Books Exploring Psychology Through the Lens of Faith

- **Source**: Home of a Book Lover
- **Focus**: Curated list of books that bridge psychology and spiritual wisdom.
- **Highlights**:
- Includes works by Viktor Frankl, Carl Jung, and contemporary thinkers
- Covers themes like meaning-making, suffering, and spiritual growth
- Ideal for readers seeking both academic and personal insight
- Explore the list

Topics You Might Explore Further

- **Attachment theory and faith development** (John Bowlby, Erik Erikson)
- **Self-compassion and spiritual healing** (Kristin Neff)
- **Awe and transcendence psychology** (Dacher Keltner, Jonathan Haidt)

- **Post-traumatic growth and meaning-making** (Viktor Frankl, Richard Tedeschi)

- **Mindfulness and contemplative practices** (Jon Kabat-Zinn, Thich Nhat Hanh)

Also by BernsPen

Sanctum

Sanctum Vol.2: The Gospel of Humanity

When God Was a Blueprint

When God Was a Blueprint

When God Was a Blueprint: The Root Protocol

Standalone

EL PASADO: Some Art Should Remain Undisturbed

The Balintataw Oracle

Decoding Faith: Bridging Divides, Reclaiming Meaning, and Navigating a Post-Truth Era

Decoding Jesus: Timeless Wisdom for a Modern Life

Divine Algorithm: Science, Spirituality, and the Search for Ultimate Reality

The Gift

The Antichrist: In the Paradox of Faith

The Seventh Deception

Lanterns in the Dark: Life Lessons for a Changing World

The Quiet Siege

The Five Trials
The Last Conversation
One Month and Two Days After
The Last Maestro
The Man Who Failed to Move
Morning at Fernando's Road
The Girl With a Panda Lunchbox
The River Remembers
Through the Quiet Wall
Bean Curd Philosophy
Sanctum
Sulit Meal: The AI Retribution
Pito-Pito: The Seven-Leaf Secret
Moony
An Old School Musician's View On the Integration of AI in Music Creation
Sometimes We Messed Up
The Destiny Blueprint: Discover Your True Purpose
Time-Eaters
The Adrenalin in Red and Blue
Venom
Spencer's Code
Concrete Eden: The Last Green Lot
The Anatomy of Faith

Watch for more at https://bernspenshorts.blogspot.com/.

About the Author

Berns Pen is a passionate explorer of ideas, driven by a desire to understand and share. His writing ventures into the profound realms of **philosophy, science, religion, psychology, and self-help**, alongside imaginative **fiction**. Each piece reflects his unique perspective on the human condition and the quest for personal growth.

Read more at https://bernspenshorts.blogspot.com/.

www.ingramcontent.com/pod-product-compliance
Lightning Source LLC
LaVergne TN
LVHW050344210926
848481LV00017B/1408
9798233030901